My heart, His ears

Angel Ragans

BookLeaf Publishing

Presentation by *BookLeaf Publishing*

Web: www.bookleafpub.com

E-mail: info@bookleafpub.com

ISBN : 9789357210447

First edition 2022

DEDICATION

"A good man leaves an inheritance to his children's children..."

To my son, Louis, if I have given nothing, taught nothing nor sacrificed a thing, may this small token ignite the God in you and make your eyes behold His wonder. You are my life, my love, my legacy

PREFACE

I don't know about you but sometimes life happens in these crashing waves of either good or bad. No matter what it is, I'm rarely ready for the billow. I have found that in these times, I'm often left without a way of expressing the overwhelming weight of the moment; however, writing poetry has proven to help when I feel helpless, without an outlet. What works even better is when I can encourage someone and glorify God while doing it. This collection of poetry is rich with ebbs and flow. Hurt, confusion, frustration, joy, concern and worship fill these pages because that's what life has been for me. It is my desire to connect with a part of you that may have had questions or have ever felt like expressing much like I have; it really is therapeutic to know that you do not walk alone. Come go with me as I reach the Father with poems from my heart directly to His ears.

HELPLESS

You are beautiful
As I gaze through the radiance of your promise,
My hopeful pupils set intrinsically ablaze
Helpless.

At Your mighty command
My stringed limbs stand
Ready for the slightest instruction, just to hear
from You.
Helpless

I worship Your majesty though the pressing mist
Of Your glorious presence paralyzes the
instrument.
Helpless

A thousand times over I will extol a wave of
surrender
Knees to neck, neck to floor
In this moment
Not a minute after or a second before
Helpless

If only these frail arms fashioned in flesh
And these feeble knees didn't require rest

I would, without end,
Bow before You Father and Friend
I would present a living offering again and again

That would be the least I could do for the Son of Man
The man God sonned
The Ancient of Days
The Most Holy One

Who could ever exalt you in a way that you deserve?
From the tiniest ants
To the largest of birds
From the utterly speechless
To the soul filled with words
It is proven impossible, Wonderful Counselor, to make You bigger
Despite the use of adjective and verb.

The complexity of whom we've discovered You to be
Is far beyond our limits, humanly.
Great God of the Universe,
You've adorned the heavens with balls of fire and
Bursts of gas.
Your many wonder works
are many too wide and plenty too vast

You are beautiful
The rolling, foaming, churning ocean agrees
With the resilient, enduring, immortal evergreen
From the rich and vivid cotton candy sky
To the exotic, endless, snow capped mountains
that all testify
Of your unimaginable, unfathomable expertise
To make the otherwise boring, explicitly
unique.

Brown, yellow, white and tan
A mere blow into the nose of your hand-made
man
Jumpstarted a creation made from the sand.
One that needs rescuing again and again.

Though man's simple yet wicked
You created a plan
A way for us to only need the blood of one lamb
To sacrifice once and for all
So that division between you and us would end
Sins absolved.

Thank You for Your beauty and for your essence
Those Fatherly attributes
We experience in Your presence.
May we ever be found in your divine favor
And under Your watchful care

Thank you for newness, wholeness, triumph, liberty and love beyond compare.

IN HER EYES

There's something in her eyes
That you may have overlooked
There's something in her eyes
Where joy was, it has been took

There's something in her eyes
In the place of peace, pain now lies
Hurt anger distress
Complete for why she didn't pass the test

You didn't know? You couldn't tell?
Her eyes had made it plain if you had looked
and looked well
Didn' t judge but gazed with care
More hurt in her eyes you could have spared

A speck to her, a beam to you
If the foot were in the other shoe
I'd tell her that she should tell you
"I love you sis and you'll make it through"

BEFORE IT'S TOO LATE

Dear Sybil, dear Destiny
I’ve a story to tell
If you’d just allow me
A moment of your time
Because time’s always key
The plot of this tale is
not known very well
but needed none the less
I confess
One not lost on… me

There once was a girl most prettiest of sorts
Intelligent and kind and she even played sports
She’d have all she wanted, all her heart desired
But what she wanted most-her mother’s heart-
was not for hire
she acted out in school
refused to do the dishes
temper tantrums galore
but still no attention
she’d pick little fights
wear little skirts
she do little extra
but very little worked

she began to give up and look someplace else for love and attention
and indeed she'd find it, in the eyes of anxious men.
Both young and old alike,
Some more bold than more so polite
She found herself paying the piper for what she thought she's due
For if you pay one way precious girl, you'll always pay in two
Once for the ride
Two times for the rockin
Once for the thrill and twice for the pillow talkin
Once for the novacane
And thrice for more to numb the pain

But she got what she needed to ease the longing in her soul
The things her well being greeded to feed her need for control
There is so little we can steer
So little that we can choose
She'd figure that out early as she commandeered her next move
She needs to tell her at just the right time
Right after church especially if there's a prayer line
But not too late into the night
For if there's a deacon's meeting

Her attitude might not be right
So she'd watch very closely for just the perfect time
To tell her mother her period's a little behind
Maybe this will be it, maybe she'll finally see
How she needs her mother's stewardship to finally breath

But it didn't happen in anyway how she planned
In fact when she came to, across her face was her mother's hand
Ringing in her ears
the hatred was very clear
and what she'd known about God was incorrect, she'd always feared
He is not a God of love
His kindness is limited
His concern-indifferent
Forget about grace
It's something to be earned
In it's proper time
And in it's proper place
He's looking low-low
And writing way long
He doesn't care how sorry you are
And how you say you are wrong

Her mother hated her, a reflection of His love

So into the arms of the enemy, she and her baby were shoved
She was inconsolable, nothing made sense
They told her Jesus loved her, why wouldn't mother recompense

Her child's father would offer relief if any were to be had
It was temporary and fleeting, methamphetamine had a grasp
The days became a blur and all ran as one
She barely remembered her name
To addiction she had succumb.

She almost lost the baby and her life just the same
But God had a plan for a witness to pray
That she'd know His glory and treasure His truth
That no matter what she'd done, he'd never let loose
Of His care for her and concern for her baby
No might be, or could be, no if, ands or maybe's.

She believed every truth the stranger would tell
And every lie of the devil she sent straight back to hell.
The lie she wasn't good enough to ever be loved
The lie that she'd done too much for God to think of

Her as a daughter, a princess, a diamond in the rough
A warrior and queen a true modern Deborah.

I wish I could tell you her mother straightened up
That she finally got saved and exemplified God's love
But honestly she couldn't-Her heart was too corrupt
She too had been neglected and how she cared was only a reflection
Of her own desires laid waste of kindness and protection
What she did was what she knew
And what she didn't do
she didn't know she's supposed to

you see, what we give is what we get
and what we get sometime's not legit.
So be careful what you reciprocate
Mother's have the power to bend, mend or make
Just like the almighty Lord
You'll get it back if you've correctly poured
Into the heart of a young hand maiden
She sees God in you even when you're heavy laiden

The young woman grew to be a mighty woman of God
She got cleaned up and quickly she found a job
She left her child's father and reached for God's best
It was in the scripture she'd learn How He would invest
In her by the sacrifice of His only begotten son
No more acting out
No more drugs
She was officially done
With trying to be accepted
Because she already was
By her daddy God looking down on her from up above
It would prove to be a long road
Sometimes tedious
But always worth it
considering her need for Jesus

Her young child grew to be
a young woman who'd soon see
the work raising a young woman would be

Her daughter's, daughter too
fought to be seen
a devilment brew
the worst you'd ever dream
but the mother of the daughter

prayers stayed going up to the father
every generational curse would be cursed
with a curse and go not one inch further
They were purchased with new blood
No matter how the enemy came in like a flood

You may wonder how I know so well the tale
of this youngling and mommy
Because the loveless little girl was none but me

So I write to tell you to please tread lightly.
Fight for your child and for your family
Because the enemy only wants to fight her
constantly
To steal her peace and wreck her mind
To cause her to wander completely blind
His desire is to sift her faith
And cause premature destruction
But the battle is not ours
Jesus causes us to win

Pray for your baby
Never give up
Lay prostate before God
Let him fill your empty cups
Look your girl deeply in her eyes
Tell her of the beauty of God that lies
In the depths of her heart
Where the issues of life can stop or start

Her destiny and preordained plan
Tell her that nothing is worth that
especially no one man
tell her of the beauty of her glowing skin
and sparkling spirit
tell her again and again
that God truly blessed her with indescribable strength
that there is nothing she can't do when God's in the center of it

Tell your young lady that you love her
better yet, show it
when you run your hand gently across her face
to lower it
to catch her chin
and a glimpse of her soul
so your eyes are not strangers and
communication is opened
so she'll tell you anything and everything
and though it's scary
it will be before she prematurely marries
it will be before an unplanned baby
because she'll wait
it will be before addiction
because cool is not just drugs to take
it will be before bitterness and resentment
it will be before maternal heart break

most importantly, dear daughter, it will all be
before it's too late

BETTER IS THE END OF A THING

This is just the beginning
This is just the beginning
This is just the beginning

If you are having a hard time remembering or thinking
There was a time your were undeniably sinking
You know, when hope was less
A whisper in your ear said "t'is only a test"

What about when you should have died
Somehow, someway you made it out alive
And it wasn't of your own power or might
It was the love of a savior-refused to let you out of His sight
It was the strong arm of a Father, cradling you
His peace and spirit physically enabling through
The toughest parts of your life
Reminding that you can do all things through christ

This is another one of those moments where the going is tough

But it's only the beginning, you been through
worse stuff
Hold your head up
and your heart steady
As you quietly wait for God to be ready
To burst open the door of new chances
When all of his promises are soon granted

If you can but hold on a little bit further
You'll be able to testify of another pre cursor
To God's unfailing plan for you
The enemy tries to steal the truth
Lesser is he than God's greater in you

No matter where you find yourself at this
moment in time
Sit back, relax and in His peace you'll abide
Rest In the bosom of God's blessings found in
His Word
Where He often gifts answers to prayers unheard

GRATEFULLY YOURS

When my back was against the wall
 I had nowhere to turn, I had given my all and all
Thank You for saving me.

When I chose to leave You,
to do my own thing,
The choices were few
Thank You for saving me.

When I gave in to the devil and his trap
I was hurting
You called me back
Thank You for saving me.

I willingly said no to Your will
Had the nerve to cry out
You accepted me still
Thank You for saving me.

When I felt like there was no way out
No way to deal
You touched my face
Wiped away the tears
My heart you healed.

You kissed my bruises my bumps, my scars
My spiritual gashes
My slits and stitches
You saved me from the caskets

I'll tell everyone of what Your son's done
For them and for me too
I'll love Your saints with dedication
That's what I'll do for You
For I'll prove that I'm grateful for salvation

DARK

Dark as a an onyx stone sitting at attention
On the right ring finger of a fiance's in
suspension

Dark as the dawn without a next day to mention

Dark as a woman's mind led solely by intuition

Dark as a long list of needs
Dark as the short means of ease

Dark as the longing to fulfill
Dark as the self limiting thrill

Dark as a life bound by death, hell and the grave

Dark as a soul left without a savior to save

Dark as a hope deferred, a heart made sick

From a desire so deep, one's left empty without
it

Dark is real trouble in a true paradise

Running with a single thought, when one should think twice

Dark as when all's well that end's well
But you wind up saying goodbyes, adieus and farewells

Dark is an unfortunate fumble when it was had in a bag

It's when one thought they had plenty but now's down to the last.

If you know the feeling of this dismal abyss
You understand the eternal void that one cannot dismiss

The overwhelming desire to be set free
From journeying in circles, left only incomplete

If you know then you know and
If you don't then you won't
But if you can, here's the plan
You are flesh of His flesh and bone of his bone
Wrapped himself in man, for your sins he's atoned

He's given you what to desire so that you may delight

Listen closely as he navigates through the day
and through the night

A city sat on a hill, you are to be the light
no matter how dark it gets
He's equipped you with his Word, his life and
his holy spirit.

THE QUESTIONS

Why me?
the motherlode of questions that oft come up
billions of people, why for me is life so tough
why do the wicked prosper while I struggle
without end
why is it always someone else's time and time
for me just starts again
The answer?
because to whom much is given, much is
required
what is on the inside of you's nothing short of
being admired
if you don't go through, you can never get to
to appreciate the journey God must mold you
it is in the shaping that one's true self can be
found
It is in the master's hands all reasoning is sound
Trust the path, even when the math don't math
Trust the course, even when it all feels forced.

When?
Patience is a virtue, something they say
Until they are on the other side of that said wait
How is it one forms this question
when our Father lives Outside of time,

for time is just a construction.
He orchestrates it, bends it and manipulates it
He molds it in the palms of His hands, He is not bound by it
So when we ask when, the answer is easy, no debate
To Father God, one day is as a thousand years
And a thousand years, as one day
It will happen when we stop watching a pot of water
Waiting for it to boil, just when we surrender to the potter
The enemy's plan will foil,
we will plunder, loot, and take all the spoils in
Not if but when the victory's given

What is happening?
A refining
Just like silver and gold
When it's all said and has all been told,
revealed will be a new defining
Of an old idea of you,
Jesus said it best, "behold i make all things new"
Old things will pass away
No longer subjected to what others say
And how others feel.
You will operate in the fullness of Christ
In you, He will be revealed
What a moment to stand in confidence

Knowing the shedding of your old self is the evidence
Of a fatih that boldly declares
Jesus is Lord and the enemy is scared
Of that moment when you lay hold of your purpose and calling
He knows the word and the word sends him crawling
Back to the pits of hell to which he will forever be
Limited by the constraints of an eternal, infernal grave that's fiery.

So Take heart,
hold peace,
get dressed
Stand still
The Word's your relief

T'is common to have questions and invited in fact
By our loving Father who wants to give feedback
To offer audible answers and instant relief
But not in place of a faith that reassures that we believe
No matter what, no matter when no matter why
Can you say: "I trust You, Lord, even if You never reply"?

DON'T CALL ME A SINNER

I may commit sin, but don't you dare call me a sinner
You have no heaven or hell to put me in
Can't call me a loser or a winner

I once was lost but now I've been found
By the son of God who wouldn't stay in the ground
I confessed my sins to Him because that's what He said to do
I laid my past before Him and His blood flows through and through

So who are you to cast a judgemental light

On my second chance, my new life?

And yes, I confessed Him as my victor and Savior
then turned around and cussed out my ex, the One I once prayed for
But conviction flooded my heart and on my knees I found myself bent

Crying before my one true love hoping it's time well spent
That He forgives me for a quick temper as I study temperance
May He change my heart and mind, offer thorough deliverance

Then there was that time I couldn't imagine going to work
So instead of calling out sick i made the lie alot worse.
I claimed a death in the family, poor Uncle Hersh.
All liars will have their place in hell
But I knew how to lie then and I still know how to tell one well
This old flesh just will not die
No matter how long and how hard I may try.

Face to the ground, heart on my sleeve
I cry out to the Lord, I beg and I plead
For the love of all things holy, forgive and change me!
As I dry my face and clear my snot
I hear His spirit reveal the plot:
The lie, the cuss, the eye roll or even drink, it matters not
What holds true, what connects the link is I'm all you've got

Simply put: you cannot live holy without my training
You will fail and fail well when you try abstaining
Let my spirit flow through you, enabling this life you surrender to me
There is levels to this, you will grow degree by degree.
But take heart in this, you have been saved by me
You will not find your past as your current identity.
You once were lost, you once were dead to sin
But no longer bound, death, hell and the grave has it's end
Watch what beautiful things happen
When into my grace you are able to tap in
When you can watch and observe growth
You become empowered by the Holyghost
To keep growing in my image, the way I made you
You'll look up one day and won't be able to find the old news
The past ques
The false truths
You'll move from glory to glory and more sin you will refuse

So when you point your trigger finger at me

You directly contradict romans 6:23
I once identified with sin
I once was a slave to it
I once was bound
I once was lost
Now im found
Now im free
New identity
In christ and Christ in me
Though I fall, falter and mistake
The truth is making me free day by day
You can call me black, ugly other than slender
But don't you part your lips to call me a sinner!

BETTER BROKEN

I'm better broken
truer words never spoken
though shattered & torn
I can still be reborn
infuse me with Gold
for riches untold
KINTSUGI

WHEN WORDS FAIL

If I were to include:
Conveying my own sorrow, ensuring my
presence tomorrow, sending my condolences,
this would never do.

I don't know what could ever be said when a
hurt this heavy has been had. I've tried it
mathematically and it just doesn't add…

I'm Sorry is:
One contraction plus one word making three
words turned two, ending with
Two words
Equaling…
Too. Few.

So, I'm sending you, in your time of need,
something greater than my sympathy.
I'm sending for your pain's relief, Isaiah 61:3.

For the heartache, the headache and feelings of
helplessness; the words of our Savior expresses
it best:

Blessed are they that mourn for they will be comforted.

With that being said, saying not much at all
To our heavenly father, Christ Savior I'll call
Interceding and praying; pushing a plate back or two
Releasing God's promises
May His peace be unto you.

THE GREAT FALL

LORD! LORD! LORD!
It hurts, It's hard, I'm torn
Tired, weak and worn
Of my self inflicted
Need for repentant
God forbidden mourn
Morning after
Weeping disaster
How long will I forlorn

Seeping laughter
My joy is now
Forever it's down
It's consequently
gone

Incidentally You came to get me
Once again reborn
No never will I
Let the devil's disguise
Trick and put one over on

Now I praise in the face of disgrace
Not bound by the thoughts of old days
Free to live in surrender

As the enemy’s choice one contender
He should have dead me
At once when he had me
Too late
I’m having devil for dinner

FOR YOU...

For You I will…
Bend my will to conform to Yours
Transform the more to prove the score's
Always with You, reigning victor

For You I will…
Commit to being an integral part of Your bride
Laying down my desires to pursue without pride
The person You've created and chosen me to be
Cause' of this same fold You've called other
sheep

For You I will
Ask, knock and continuously seek for truth
In intimacy, there's nothing I'll keep from You
I'll claw through ruthless thoughts that fight for
attention
As I kneel before a most Holy God, my spirit
remains in suspension
Waiting, watching anticipating
A word from my Lord, emancipating
My mind from a perpetual motion machine
I desire is to think of You, and think of You only

For You I will

Present my body a living sacrifice
You ask of me to be holy and live sanctified
For You I pledge to comply, it is the least I can do
You laid down Your life, the ultimate follow through
I will lay my flesh on the altar and crucify it everyday
As You perfect the work You began in me when I see You face to face

For You I will
Clothe those with no clothing
Feed those that are hungry
Give drink to those that are thirsty
in keeping Your sacred covenant,
I'll prove to You I love thee
I will look after the fatherless and unmarried
This does not compare to Your cross, but You can consider it carried

For You I will
Break my own heart over and over again
As I wait for my desire for a husband & friend
Refusing to step out of Your way to get my own
T'is only for a moment but lasts forever long
I tried it
Didn't work
I'm devoted to You, Father

Even when it hurts
I offer a tattered heart
Although, made of flesh
Remake and remold of it what's left
To reflect only Your most beautiful self
You created me in Your image
To You I'm committed
I surrender to the process

HEAVEN & HURT

I just now realized
Everyone has a voice that cries
"How"
"Why"
With our heads bowed and hands clasped
It's hard to understand
Hard to grasp
Why so much pain?
Why so much hurt?
I pray,Lord,
I go to church
Cry out 'til I'm drained
For lost souls I search
So that they know you remain
Still and always will
Eternal life
Face to face
With his grace
It's a package deal

THROWING

The bright, vibrant color of His love fills in the
spaces of shattered heart break. The potter
carefully hand crafts beautifully placed
shimmer to consume cracks and splinters.
He gently folds constant tender care into even
the dullest and darkest hurts, allowing the flash
and luster of His luminescence to accentuate the
great
The softest whisper of His Word gently primes
the subject
Finishing touches but no, not quite done yet.
The sweet aroma of a sacrifice both potter and
clay
Arrests the will, compels and stills the
complications of human nature
Nestled into form designed, chiseled, heat
blasted and wrestled
Proves to be
the refining needed to transform impurity
Poured upon the earthenware at hand
Is the reflective recipe
to reveal the master plan:
made in His image.

WHO KNEW?

Who would have thought?
Who would have knew
Who had an inkling
Who had a clue?
That one day I'd be His
One day like outta the blue
He'd call me home
Like pig calling suuuuuuu
I'd come back running
tears in my eyes
I thought you'd left me
after all of my pride
You should have gone
Why did you stay?
Why didn't you leave me
Now you'll see me this way
I wanted to be better before I came back
But you never left
So much shame in the fact
You've always been good
All of the time
And all of the time
Didn't get what I should
Your grace was sufficient, mercy was strong

Shielding and covering in the midst of my
wrong.
Who could imagine?
Imagine such love
None but the Father could fathom His touch

THE MEANING OF A THING

The meaning of a thing
Is in the space that lies between
The past and the present
The moment when
Life would bend
Creating ugly or pleasant
Whichever the two
It's completely up to who
Twists and dresses it
It is at the crossroads just past the split
Awaiting your decision
To reveal itself in it
You'll find it precisely when not one thing makes sense
When you need something bigger than you to count up the expense
Pull up a chair
It's waiting there
To unfold the suspense

ATROPHY

Before you stay and waste away out of sheer loyalty
Be sure to factor in
nobody wins
in this life lottery
It's a gamble to stay and a gamble to leave
Lingering and loitering could cause atrophy
A loss
A loss of muscle
A loss of muscle mass
It's hard to grasp
The weight of a delay
Time will pass
No longer amassed
Your purpose will fade away
A loss
A loss of power
A loss of power & strength
The true will of God will diminish
Causing one not to begin nor finish
Jesus is
Jesus is coming back
Jesus is coming back for a church without spot or blemish
Listen and stay in tune with the Holy Spirit

His leading will tell you when to walk, then
walk in it
Bloom where the opportunity has been granted
and discern when it is time to be replanted

BLISS

What is this
Some call it bliss
It can be ignorance
your loves first kiss
Or your loves last miss
Cannot be a formality one just can’t resist
Sheer joy
Perfect happiness
The moment one realized
T’wasn’t always like this
Although you can’t quite remember the problem with it
God’s best work is done in the moments before you threw in the towel
Gave up on the score
The best part is
You don’t realize it
Til’ you look back & reflect on how He did it again

GOD'S GOT THIS

Hold on to God's unchanging hand
As He walks you through this life marked by
sands
Of time
Time will stand still
Outside of His will
Be sure to trust Him no matter the thrill
Guaranteed to be fleeting
And left with the bleeding
You'll look at the carnage
wish you weren't just repeating
The sins of the saints that warned with this
greeting:
"Don't let the devil ride
If he rides, he'll wanna drive"
If you leave all things to the lover of your soul
He'll make it all good, cause your destiny's
foretold
You've been called, chosen and justified
It's just as if you'd never messed up or lied
To tell you the truth
You've also been glorified
Past tense
It's already done
Not sin sick

Father, Holy Spirit and son
Sealed it with a kiss
You can sit back and relax now
GOD'S GOT THIS

BLACK

My skin is Covered and dripping and tinted
mocha melanin
My hair is kinky and curly my smile safe and
sanguine
My teeth milky white shining through the cage
of my half cocked grin
My flesh is tight-keeps me youthful
and my dark skinned Kin is as the sand of the
sea-beautiful
My cheekbones-as high as the sun in the sky
As all outdoors, my nose is wide
It hovers over my bountiful, full lips
I am woman hear me roar as I carry the nation in
my womb, the forefathers on my hip
The rhythm of the earth rides my bones as I
create a space for my son man and man son to
call home
Come rest your weary head in my rolling bosom
i'm bound to feed you till you're so full, no
room for doldrums
King, let me lift some of your load
what my shoulders can't, my heart can hold
You see, the only thing greater than my ethnicity
is the image I was made in-the God in me

IF I COULD RE-RIGHT HISTORY

If I could re-right history
From my very core, the very pit of me
I would tell Trayvon Martin: don't walk around
Don't look about, don't get too loud and don't scream and shout
No, You don't need goodies and for God's sake…
TAKE OFF THAT HOODIE!

I would tell Eric Garner: don't linger on that corner
And smoking leads to death, ask any coroner.

Mike Brown…you can't "thug out" with boys of your kind
You might murder or worse, steal to which they won't turn a blind eye

And to our poor baby Tamir Rice: it's as simple as the day: DON'T PLAY.
You know the words: black children are not to be seen and not to be heard.

I would say to Walter Scott that although it's
scary and uncertain and most times unfortunate,
DON'T RUN
It may, maybe might lead to a different outcome.

To Alton Sterling, please lay still
Don't move, don't breath, don't blink
Don't look, nor sneeze, not think.

I would say to Philando Castille: even though
you were asking for it…I mean, you were asked
for it, your driver's permit
Don't reach for a thing without permission.

And to Stephon Clark, I would say to you: no
matter how hard some try, we cannot be mute.
So to you I'd tell: don't carry a cell.

Breonna Taylor: many have fallen, fallen for the
wrong men only to wake up and try again but for
you my sister, it has proven to be the end. So to
you I'd say don't drink the Kool-aid and don't
make mistakes.

And George Floyd: watching the level of
disrespect and irreverence for human life
I'm compelled to tell you to think twice when
handling past mistakes, fugazies and fakes

Because like it or not, you're not liked and got
less than 10 minutes to live with a knee in you
neck and a blow to what's left of black citizens.

If I could re-right history
I would tell the children of the children's
children of traders that the ones their ancestors
captured were not slaves
They were priceless royalty that had been stolen
and subjected to chains.

If loose lips sink ships then I'd eagle spread the
love of Christ from wing tip to wing tip.
Because if we are really being truthful, you can't
find the love of Jesus in brutality; it's unfruitful.

I would set ablaze the endless fields of cotton
that tied the souls of my ancestors into the frame
of this America; it'd be forgotten.

Although encouragement was not needed for
many to march on in strength
I would rub and wash their cotton pickin' feet at
length.
I would walk my people to the edge of the past
right up to the threshold of the future so they
could see the wedding of their endurance and the
dream of Dr. Luther.

Oh how I would reiterate the whiting out of
falsities and lies
I would write black in and write it in black pride

I would obliterate poverty, and wash out debt
Reprogram the thought process and the entire
mindset
Even the playing field to gain some footing
When we have balance in the game, there's no
need for looting

Hopeless characters produce careless acts
So I would inject faith into the heart of every
black
And make hope contagious, no matter the
circumstance,
no matter how outrageous
Because when beaten down on so many
occasions
It begins to feel as if the devil's narrating.

If I could re-right history
The only red lining for start
would be the words of Christ that I would write
on every heart
which would influence grace and love
and disparage hateful grudge

I would write Jesus in the story of history

I would take hateful men out for centuries
And allow God to create a pure heart within us
So that together we would have more than
plenty

If I could re-right history
I would open the eyes of the blind to see
The value of black and how pretty
Drips of melanin with flecks of solid gold
Within the eyes of beauty behold
The majesty
The brilliance
The fight
The resilience
The strength
The power
The presence
The refusal to cower
We are literally legends.

Since I am unable to re-write history
I will declare unto you a prophecy
That in the last days the Lord will pour out His
spirit among all flesh
And that all that was endured will be proven a
test
We will come forth as pure gold
Spotless
Blameless

With treasures untold
Not within these earthen clay jars
But to be inherited in Heaven far beyond the stars
To lay up with the Father while He erases every scar.

Of hate
Of bitterness
Of wrath
Of better-than
Of envy
Misunderstanding
Confusion
And wickedness
May His will be done here on all of earth
As it is in Heaven
Where lamb will lay with lion
And we'll fulfill all of his purposes.

Everyday that we choose to see the content of who someone is
Versus the clothes on their back or the skin that they are in
We write afresh a future where our plights can be akin
We slap the face of racial slurs and homicidal revenge

We put in It's place the audacity of prejudice and racism.
We give love a real shot and Christ a most holy spot
In the hearts of everyone you see and who sees you.
We won't have to re-right history if we make right the right now and all move forward in victory.

www.ingramcontent.com/pod-product-compliance
Lightning Source LLC
Chambersburg PA
CBHW051736130826
49812CB00033B/887
9789357210447